MIAMI, THE MAGIC CITY

Miami was founded by Julia Tuttle, known as the "Mother of Miami." She owned 640 acres between Biscayne Bay and the Miami River. During a crop freeze in northern Florida she sent the railroad developer, Henry Flagler, perfect Miami orange blossoms and offered to deed half of her property to him if he would extend his Florida East Coast Railway and lay out a new town. He hadn't planned to go that far south, but Julia was persistent! The railroad arrived in April 1896 and the City of Miami was incorporated on July 28 that same year. Flagler became known as the "Father of Miami."

The city is bordered by two unique national parks: Everglades National Park, nicknamed "the River of Grass" by its greatest advocate, Marjory Stoneman Douglas, and Biscayne National Park, the aquatic home to beautiful coral reefs and emerald islands.

With an average annual daily temperature of 76 degrees, year-round sunshine, and world-class beaches, Miami and Miami Beach attract vacationers from all over the United States and abroad. An international city, Miami became the natural landing spot for thousands of exiled Cubans and is home to over 150 ethnicities and 60 languages, which leads to a wonderful mix of cultures, traditions, and excellent food. Miami also boasts some of the most interesting Art Deco and Mid-Century Modern (known as "MiMo") architecture in the world.

I fell in love with Miami when my family moved here in 1985. In this book, I wanted to share with my son some of the places that make the city so special, and I hope the book inspires you to do the same.

Patricia Baloyra

Goodnight MIAMI

Written by Patricia Baloyra • Illustrated by Sarah Knotz

AMP&RSAND, INC.

Chicago • New Orleans

ISBN 9781-4507-9592-0

Design
David Robson, Robson Design

Published by
AMPERSAND, INC.
1050 North State Street
Chicago, IL 60610

203 Finland Place
New Orleans, LA 70113
www.ampersandworks.com

Printed in U.S.A.

To arrange a reading or book signing, contact the author at pbaloyra@yahoo.com

The author wishes to thank her family and friends for their support and encouragement in this endeavor. Cristina Arango, Bob de la Fuente, and JR Fry provided insight and enthusiasm every step of the way. Special thanks also to Jacqueline Arango and Stephen and Megan Weber. The author also owes a huge debt of gratitude to Suzanne Isaacs and David Robson, without whose expertise, guidance, and patience this book would not have been possible.

Special thanks to the following, who allowed use of their images for reference: Jeremy Allen, Imran Anwar, Claudia Domenig, Antonella Fava, Greater Miami Convention & Visitors Bureau, Pancho Pardo, Phillip Pessar, Suzana Profeta, Matthew F. Reyes and Gary Wolfson.

*For Sebastian, a magical boy,
born in a magical city.*

Goodnight clear blue sea. Goodnight palm trees and sand.
Goodnight big ships that cruise so far from land.

Goodnight key lime pie. Goodnight stone crabs at Joe's.

Goodnight Vizcaya. Goodnight Coconut Grove.

Goodnight black beans and rice. Goodnight plantain chips.
Goodnight to the lobsters we tickle with sticks.

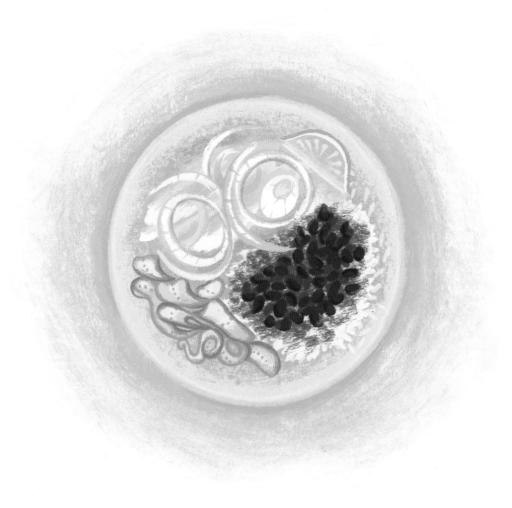

Goodnight Domino Park. Goodnight Little Havana.

Goodnight to Versailles. *Cafecito mañana.*

Goodnight Heat, Canes and Marlins, our home teams we cheer.
Goodnight to our Dolphins and that one perfect year.

Goodnight swampy Everglades. Goodnight wild airboat rides.
Goodnight all alligators with mouths that open wide, wide, wide.

Goodnight tropical weather. Goodnight balmy nights.
Goodnight Ocean Drive. Goodnight neon lights.

Goodnight Venetian Pool.
Goodnight MiChiMu.

Goodnight Jungle Island.
Goodnight friends at the Zoo.

Goodnight historic Stiltsville. Goodnight Biscayne Bay breeze.
Goodnight dolphins and seagulls. Goodnight manatees.

Goodnight purple skies and pink clouds so pretty.
Goodnight big moon. Goodnight Magic City.

MAGICAL MIAMI

The Dante B. Fascell Port of Miami, located just east of downtown Miami on Biscayne Bay, is the port of embarkation for one out of seven of the world's CRUISE passengers.

KEY LIMES are citrus fruit with a tart flavor perfect for custard pies. Ripe key limes are actually yellow, not green!

The FLORIDA STONE CRAB is found in the shores off Miami. If it loses a limb, the stone crab can grow it back to full size within a year or two. Stone crab season runs from October 15 to May 15.

Built between 1914 and 1916, VIZCAYA is a National Historic Landmark. The bayfront Italian Renaissance villa is sited on 10 acres of formal gardens and a native hardwood forest. In 1953, it was opened to the public as a museum. For more information, visit www.vizcayamuseum.org.

COCONUT GROVE is a neighborhood south of downtown Miami, known for its marina, big trees, eclectic restaurants, quirky shops, Bahamian culture, and outdoor festivals, including the Grove Arts Festival, the King Mango Strut, the Taste of the Grove, the Goombay Festival, and the Great Grove Bed Race.

FRIJOLES NEGROS (black beans) and PLANTAIN CHIPS (*mariquitas*) are staples of Cuban cuisine.

The FLORIDA SPINY LOBSTER lives on reefs and in mangrove swamps in the waters in and around Miami. It has spiny antennae that stick out from its eyes and no front claws. Snorkelers catch lobsters by poking at them with a "tickle" stick, causing them to scurry backward into the snorkeler's net. Lobster season runs from August through January, with a "mini lobster season" on the last Wednesday and Thursday in July.

LITTLE HAVANA is a neighborhood just west of downtown Miami, stretching along SW 8th Street (the famous *Calle Ocho*), and is best known as the landing spot for many Cuban exiles. Two iconic meeting places are Maximo Gomez Park (better known as DOMINO PARK) and VERSAILLES, the World's Most Famous Cuban Restaurant. For four decades Versailles has been serving tasty Cuban cuisine, CAFECITO and culture at 3555 SW 8th St.

The MIAMI HEAT is Miami's professional basketball team. For more information or tickets, visit www.nba.com/heat.

The University of Miami, more simply "The U," is located in Coral Gables. Its sports teams are known as the Hurricanes, or "CANES." For more information or tickets, visit www.hurricanesports.com.

The MIAMI MARLINS are the city's professional baseball team. For more information or tickets, visit www.marlins.com.

The MIAMI DOLPHINS are Miami's professional football team and the only team in NFL history to complete a perfect season, posting a 17-0 record and winning the Super Bowl in the 1972 season. For more information or tickets, visit www.miamidolphins.com.

The FLORIDA EVERGLADES are subtropical wetlands, home to many species of plants and animals, including ALLIGATORS, the American crocodile, the Ibis, Key deer, and the Florida panther. You can explore the Everglades on foot, on bicycle, in a canoe or kayak or, most famously, on an AIRBOAT, which features a big fan on the back that propels the boat forward.

Running parallel to the Atlantic Ocean on Miami Beach, OCEAN DRIVE is home to a collection of pastel and neon-decorated hotels, restaurants, and nightclubs often referred to as "South Beach."

The VENETIAN POOL is a spring water pool fed from an underground aquifer, built in 1923 on the site of a former coral rock quarry. For more information or admission rates, visit www.coralgables.com/CGWeb/parks_rec_files/vp_home.aspx.

The MIAMI CHILDREN'S MUSEUM entertains and educates children in its unique building, located across Biscayne Bay from downtown Miami on Watson Island. The museum's adorable mascot is called MICHIMU. For more information or tickets, visit www.miamichildrensmuseum.org.

JUNGLE ISLAND is home to parrots, white tigers, flamingos, warm-weather penguins, a serpentarium, and a rare liger (a lion-tiger hybrid). For more information or tickets, visit www.jungleisland.com.

ZOO MIAMI features over 2,000 animals, over 40 endangered species, and over 100 exhibits on 740 acres in southern Miami-Dade County. For more information or tickets, visit www.zoomiami.org.

STILTSVILLE is a collection of seven houses built on stilts in the early 1930s in shallow water in BISCAYNE BAY. Year round, people flock to Biscayne Bay to enjoy boating, kayaking, canoeing, fishing, lobstering, jet skiing, water skiing, windsurfing and all kinds of sports and recreation on the water.

MANATEES are gentle and slow-moving gray mammals that spend most of their time eating, resting and traveling. Adults are about 10 feet long, weigh about 1,000 pounds, have a flat tail, two flippers and a large, wrinkled head. For more information, visit www.savethemanatee.org.

Miami acquired its nickname, the MAGIC CITY, as a result of its rapid growth, becoming a bustling metropolis seemingly overnight.

ABOUT THE AUTHOR

Patricia Baloyra is a land use and zoning attorney with a law degree from the University of Pennsylvania and a B.A. from the University of Miami. She lives in Miami with her partner, Cristina, their son Sebastian, and their pets, Rocco and Leo.

ABOUT THE ILLUSTRATOR

Sarah Knotz is a graphic artist based in Brooklyn, New York. She studied graphic design at the Rhode Island School of Design before pursuing her M.F.A. in illustration at the School of Visual Arts. She draws inspiration for her work from travel, music, reading, and watching the seasons change in New York City.